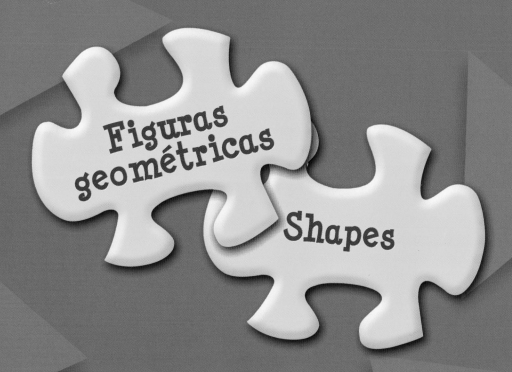

Figuras geométricas

Shapes

Triángulos/Triangles

por/by Sarah L. Schuette

Traducción/Translation: Dr. Martín Luis Guzmán Ferrer

Asesora literaria/Reading Consultant:

Dra. Elena Bodrova, asesora principal/Senior Consultant

Mid-continent Research for Education and Learning

A+ books

BILINGÜE/BILINGUAL

CAPSTONE PRESS
a capstone imprint

A+ Books are published by Capstone Press,
151 Good Counsel Drive, P.O. Box 669, Mankato, Minnesota 56002.
www.capstonepress.com

092009
005620LKS10

Library of Congress Cataloging-in-Publication Data
Schuette, Sarah L., 1976–
    [Triangles. Spanish & English]
    Triángulos : triángulos a nuestro alrededor = Triangles : seeing triangles all around us /
por Sarah L. Schuette.
    p. cm. — (A+ bilingüe. Figuras geométricas = A+ bilingual. Shapes)
    Summary: "Simple text, photographs, and illustrations show triangles in everyday objects — in both
English and Spanish" — Provided by publisher.
    Includes index.
    ISBN 978-1-4296-4589-8 (lib. bdg.)
    1. Triangle — Juvenile literature. I. Title. II. Title: Triangles : seeing triangles all around us.
III. Series.
QA482.S38518 2010
516'.154 — dc22   2009040929

Created by the A+ Team

Sarah L. Schuette, editor; Katy Kudela, bilingual editor; Adalin Torres-Zayas, Spanish copy editor;
    Heather Kindseth, art director and designer; Jason Knudson, designer and illustrator;
    Angi Gahler, illustrator; Gary Sundermeyer, photographer; Nancy White, photo stylist;
    Eric Manske, production specialist

Note to Parents, Teachers, and Librarians

The Figuras geométricas/Shapes series uses color photographs and a nonfiction format to introduce
children to the shapes around them in both English and Spanish. It is designed to be read aloud
to a pre-reader or to be read independently by an early reader. The images help early readers and
listeners understand the text and concepts discussed. The book encourages further learning by
including the following sections: Table of Contents, Glossary, Internet Sites, and Index. Early readers
may need assistance using these features.

Table of Contents/
Tabla de contenidos

Playing with Triangles   4
What Triangles Do   8
Eating Triangles   16
More Triangles   24
Play Triangle Toss   28
Glossary   30
Internet Sites   30
Index   32

▼ ▲ ▼ ▲ ▼ ▲ ▼ ▲ ▼ ▲ ▼ ▲

Vamos a jugar con triángulos   4
Qué hacen los triángulos   8
Comamos triángulos   16
Más triángulos   24
Vamos a jugar a lanzar el triángulo   28
Glosario   31
Sitios de Internet   31
Índice   32

Triangles have three sides and are flat.

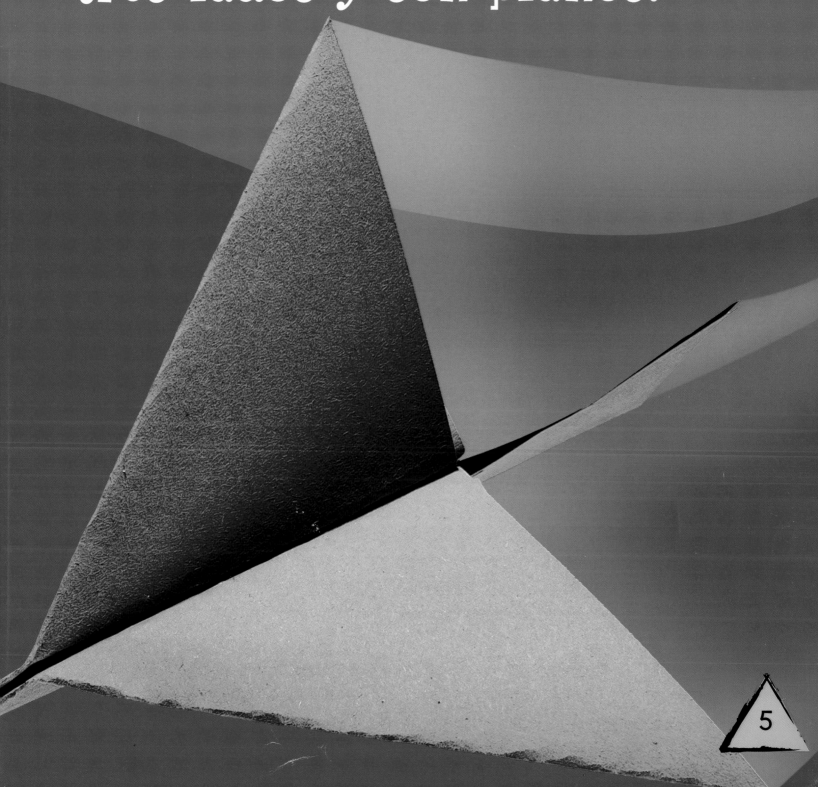

Los triángulos tienen
tres lados y son planos.

5

Triangles can even
be food for a cat.

▼ ▲ ▼ ▲ ▼ ▲ ▼ ▲ ▼ ▲ ▼ ▲

Los triángulos pueden
ser hasta la comida
para el gato.

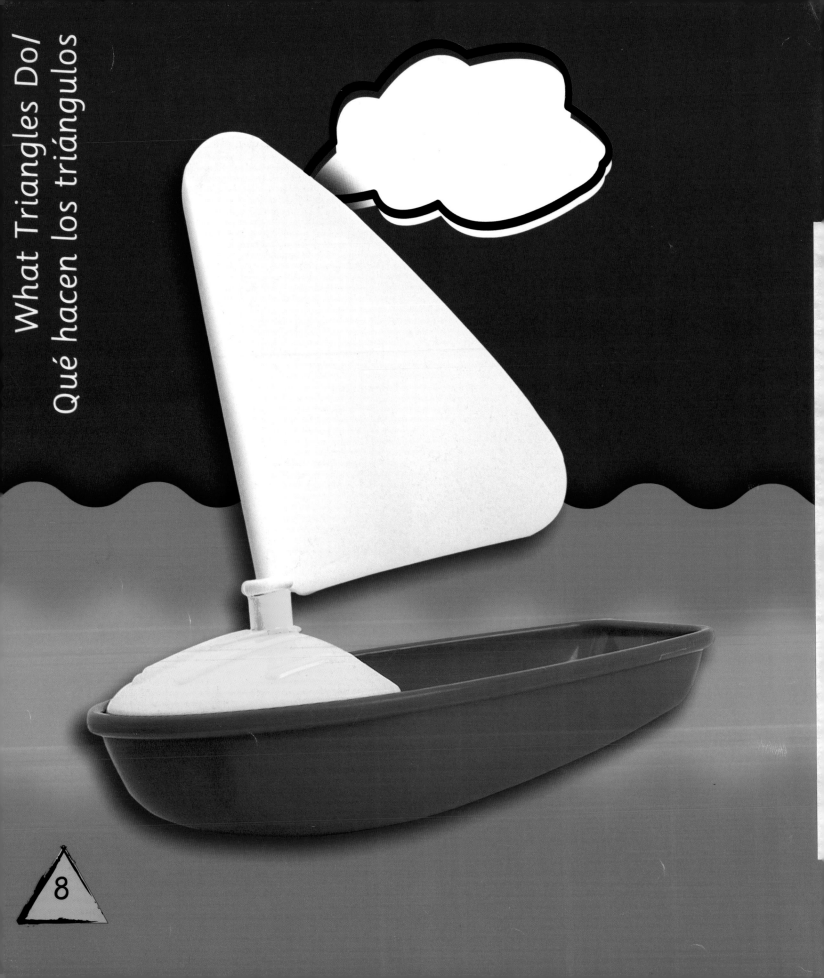

8

Boats use sails to move. The sails catch the wind. Wind pushes the boat along the water.

Los barcos usan velas para moverse. Las velas atrapan el viento. El viento empuja al barco en el agua.

Sails are triangles on a boat.

▼ ▲ ▼ ▲ ▼ ▲ ▼ ▲ ▼ ▲

Las velas son triángulos en un barco.

9

Buttons keep shirts, coats, and other clothing closed. The buttons slide into buttonholes.

Los botones son para cerrar los abrigos, las camisas y otras prendas. Los botones se meten en los ojales.

These triangles close up a coat.

Estos triángulos cierran el abrigo.

11

A triangle patch stays on with thread.

Un parche en forma de triángulo se queda pegado con hilo.

13

Go Te
Cou

14

Team triangles are blue and red.

Los banderines de los equipos deportivos son triángulos azules y rojos.

15

16

Some triangles are
juicy and sweet.

Your body is made mostly of water just like a watermelon. Water helps to make watermelons juicy. You can eat every part of a watermelon, even the seeds and the rind.

Tu cuerpo está hecho de agua en gran parte tal como una sandía. El agua hace que las sandías sean jugosas. Puedes comerte todas las partes de la sandía, hasta las semillas y la cáscara.

Algunos triángulos son dulces y jugosos.

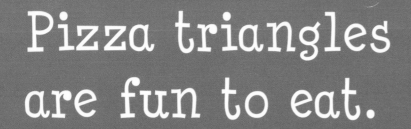

Pizza triangles
are fun to eat.

Los triángulos de la
pizza son divertidos
de comer.

18

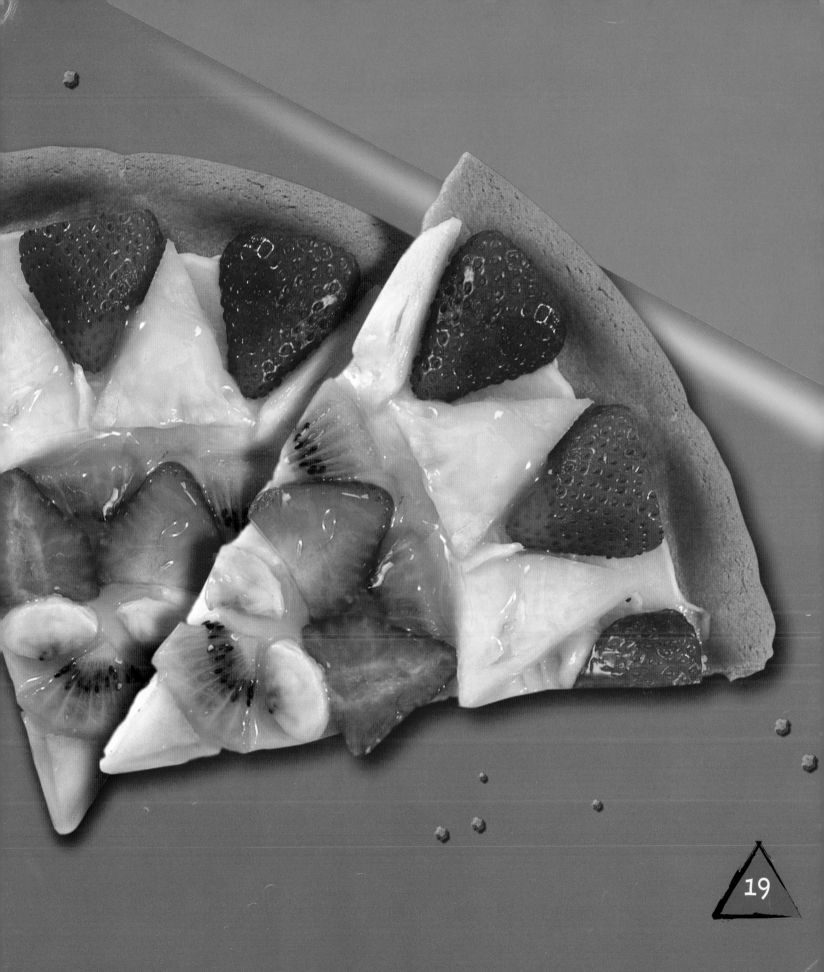

Bite these triangles
and hear a crunch.

▼ ▲ ▼ ▲ ▼ ▲ ▼ ▲ ▼ ▲ ▼ ▲

Muerde estos triángulos
y verás como crujen.

20

21

You can cut one square in half
to make two triangles.

Puedes partir un cuadrado
a la mitad para hacer
dos triángulos.

You might find triangles
in your lunch.

Puede que encuentres
triángulos en tu comida.

23

Some signs have arrows. The arrows are triangles that tell people which way to go. Other signs are triangles that tell people to watch out.

Algunas señales tienen flechas. Las flechas son triángulos que indican a las personas en qué dirección ir. Otras señales son triángulos que indican a las personas que tengan cuidado.

Triangles point to the left and to the right.

Los triángulos
señalan a la izquierda
o a la derecha.

Which triangle is
shiny and bright?

¿Cuál de estos triángulos
es brillante y luminoso?

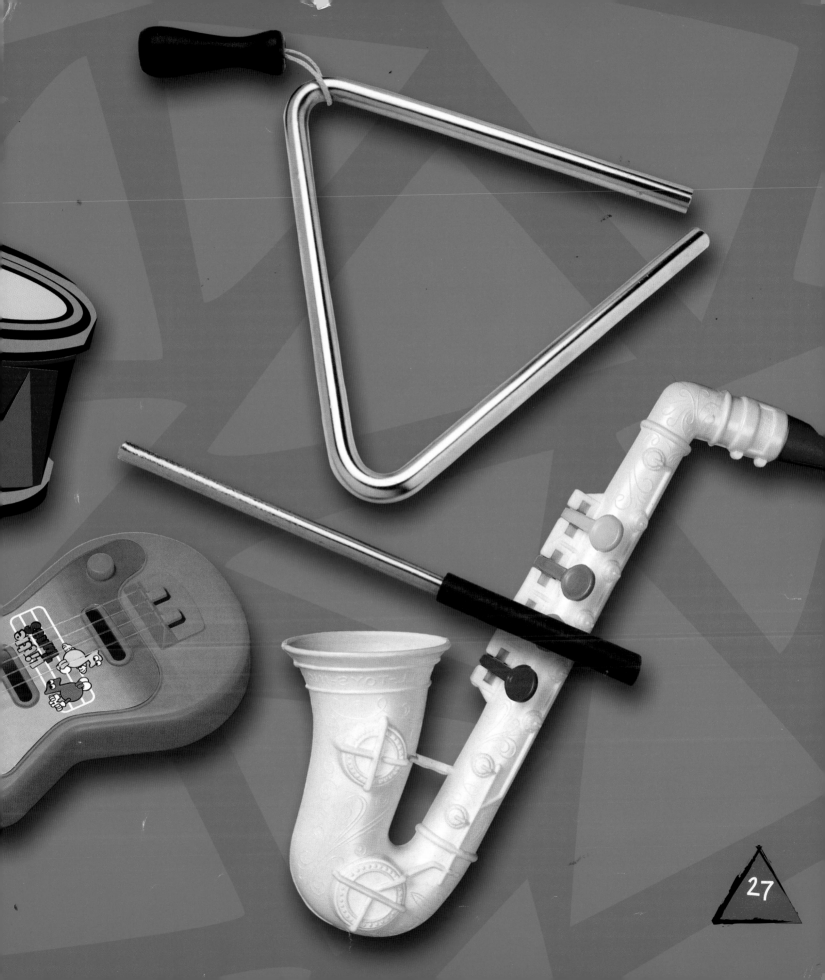

Play Triangle Toss/ Vamos a jugar a lanzar el triángulo

You will need/ Necesitas:

drinking straws/
pajillas

scissors/
tijeras

yarn/
una bola de hilo

ruler/
una regla

drinking cup/
un vasito de agua

friends/
y a tus amigos

28

1 Cut off the bottom of three straws below the bend. It takes three straw pieces to make one triangle.

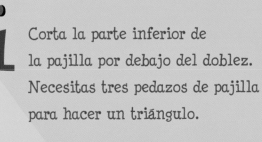

1 Corta la parte inferior de la pajilla por debajo del doblez. Necesitas tres pedazos de pajilla para hacer un triángulo.

2 Cut one 24-inch (60-centimeter) piece of yarn. Thread the yarn through all three pieces of straw. Tie together to make a triangle. Trim the ends of the yarn with a scissors. Repeat Steps 1 and 2 to make three triangles for each player.

2 Corta un pedazo de hilo de 24 pulgadas (60 centímetros). Pasa el hilo por los tres pedazos de pajilla. Amárralos para hacer un triángulo. Recorta las puntas del hilo con las tijeras. Repite los pasos 1 y 2 hasta hacer tres triángulos para cada jugador.

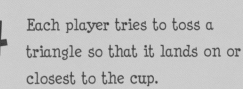

3 Place the cup upside down in the middle of a room. Have your friends stand about 4 feet (1.2 meters) away from the cup.

3 Coloca el vaso de cabeza en el centro de una habitación. Haz que tus amigos se pongan como a 4 pies (1.2 metros) del vaso.

4 Each player tries to toss a triangle so that it lands on or closest to the cup.

4 Cada jugador intenta lanzar el triángulo para que caiga en el vaso o lo más cerca posible.

Glossary

rind — the tough outer layer on melons, citrus fruits, and some cheeses; watermelon rinds are smooth and hard.

sail — a large sheet of strong cloth such as canvas that makes a boat move when it catches the wind; some sails are triangular in shape.

seed — the part of a flowering plant that can grow into a new plant; watermelons have black and white seeds.

thread — a strand of cotton or other material used for sewing; people sew patches on clothing to cover holes or stains.

Internet Sites

FactHound offers a safe, fun way to find Internet sites related to this book. All of the sites on FactHound have been researched by our staff.

Here's all you do:

Visit *www.facthound.com*

FactHound will fetch the best sites for you!

Glosario

la cáscara — capa exterior dura de los melones, cítricos y algunos quesos; las cáscaras de los melones son lisas y duras.

el hilo — hebra de algodón u otro material que se usa para coser; las personas cosen parches en la ropa para tapar agujeros o manchas.

la semilla — parte de una planta que florece y puede convertirse en una planta nueva; los melones tienen semillas negras y blancas.

la vela — sábana de tela fuerte como la lona que hace que un barco se mueva cuando atrapa al viento; algunas velas tienen forma triangular.

Sitios de Internet

FactHound brinda una forma segura y divertida de encontrar sitios de Internet relacionados con este libro. Todos los sitios en FactHound han sido investigados por nuestro personal.

Esto es todo lo que tú necesitas hacer:

Visita *www.facthound.com*

¡FactHound buscará los mejores sitios para ti!

Index

arrows, 24
boat, 9
buttons, 11
cat, 7
coat, 11
left, 24
lunch, 23
patch, 12
pizza, 18

right, 24
rind, 17
sails, 9
seeds, 17
signs, 24
thread, 12
water, 9, 17
watermelon, 17

Índice

abrigo, 11
agua, 9, 17
barco, 9
botones, 11
cáscara, 17
comida, 23
derecha, 25
flechas, 24
gato, 7

hilo, 12
izquierda, 25
parche, 12
pizza, 18
sandía, 17
semillas, 17
señales, 24
velas, 9

32